Inspired Poems

INSPIRED POEMS

Glenn Thrush

All my best
Glenn (Bill) Thrush

iUniverse, Inc.
New York Lincoln Shanghai

Inspired Poems

Copyright © 2007 by Glenn W. Thrush

All rights reserved. No part of this book may be used or reproduced by any means, graphic, electronic, or mechanical, including photocopying, recording, taping or by any information storage retrieval system without the written permission of the publisher except in the case of brief quotations embodied in critical articles and reviews.

iUniverse books may be ordered through booksellers or by contacting:

iUniverse
2021 Pine Lake Road, Suite 100
Lincoln, NE 68512
www.iuniverse.com
1-800-Authors (1-800-288-4677)

Because of the dynamic nature of the Internet, any Web addresses or links contained in this book may have changed since publication and may no longer be valid.

The views expressed in this work are solely those of the author and do not necessarily reflect the views of the publisher, and the publisher hereby disclaims any responsibility for them.

ISBN: 978-0-595-45333-7 (pbk)
ISBN: 978-0-595-89646-2 (ebk)

Printed in the United States of America

Contents

Earth and Ethereal 1
The Snowbird 2
In the mall 3
White Elephant 4
Smoke Alarm 5
Popcorn 6
Alabama 7
Finances.... ugh! 8
First Christmas Poem: 1978 9
Car Repair 10
Sand and Sea 11
Absolutes: no explanation needed 12
Wake Forest 13
Out on the Range 14
A world without coffee 15
The black widow spider. 16
Reunion 17
Christmas Comes 18
The Tadpole 19
The Grocery Store 20
A special Anniversary 21
When I was a little critter.... 22

A Cookie 23
Puffins? 24
My wife likes the comics and so 25
Another mall poem..... 26
Taxes 27
Clumsy Friend—broken arm 28
Came the Wisemen 29
Thanksgiving 30
A Valentine to Sue 31
For Mother's Day 32
A Valentine 33
For Father's Day 34
Daughter in Ohio—freezing 35
Any lady who has had a small kitchen.... 36
Hannukka 37
Memorial 38
Decision 39
Christmas Friendship 40
Lights are on the Christmas tree 41
Christmas Present Time 42
Merry Christmas in '92 43
As we near the Christmas Day 44
It's time to celebrate 45
Onward they trudged 46
The night was cold 47
Jesus was born 48
Under a star 49

Jesus lives on Earth 50
He came to us 51
Jesus lives in Heaven 52
What is more free 53
Jesus came 54
Remember 9-11-01 55

Earth and Ethereal

In my earthly being and in my earthly time
I want to be in a good place
As a poet, I want to make it rhyme
I don't want bars on my windows
And I don't want bars on my doors
I don't want to fight with my neighbors
I don't want to settle any scores
I want to live in peace with God and my fellow man
To that end I will try to do all the good I can
The commandments all are there—
They number one to ten
We should read them ten times ten a day
And read them once again
Then walk with God and Jesus until the end of time
Then we will be in heaven
And this completes my earthly rhyme.

I hope my poems will enrich your life.
    My name is Glenn Thrush

All about "snowbirds"..... .

The Snowbird

The snowbird comes and the snowbird goes
The snowbird is never in a place where it snows
The snowbird goes where the weather is nice
The snowbird is never in a place where there's ice
And so in Phoenix, this bird doth light
At a time of course, when the weather's just right
A few months later, that bird is gone
Gone up north, to mow the lawn

In the mall

The mall's a place where you can go
To shop and dream and look
Toys and clothes and records and such
You can even buy a book
Food is there of every kind
If you should wish to eat
And if you want to "people watch"
Just grab yourself a seat
Stores are there of every kind
You can even see a movie
My thoughts on the mall:
I think the mall is groovy

I was invited to a White Elephant party and so....

White Elephant

What in the world is a white elephant?
You really don't want to know
It's something that nobody wants
And it has no place to go
If you find one, say, in the lost and found
Take it home and keep it around
'cause sure as shootin' there will come a day
When someone you know will call and say,
Come to our house on Friday next week,
And bring something stupid you don't want to keep

Smoke Alarm

What would you do to save a life
Maybe your own, maybe your wife
Your husband, too, if you are a girl
So come on gang, let's give it a whirl
It's small, it's cheap, it will do no harm
Go out and buy that smoke alarm.

This one is universal. And so....

Popcorn

What is there to say about popcorn
And who can resist its charm
I have to have it in a bucket
A bucket as deep as my arm
You have to have it with butter
You have to have it with salt
If you don't get any, it's not my fault!
I've got it in my teeth
And I've got it in my hair
I spilled some on the carpet
And I spilled some in the chair
I'm all through now and I need a drink
Turn up the TV honey, and we'll be in the pink

Alabama

Alabama is great. It's great far and wide
Agriculture, mining and industry
And don't forget the Crimson Tide
Great history, great ambiance and great people
Alabama is dotted with mosque, temple and steeple
We have grit and we have grits
And don't forget the smoked "hama"
Come on ya'll, come on down to Alabama!

Finances.... ugh!

The interest rate is up the interest rate is down
The planet we live on keeps spinning around
The IRAs and the 401k
Our money is in there but should it stay
The economy is slumping we know not how far
We refinanced the house we bought a new car
Gasoline is up and the market is down
This planet we live on keeps spinning around

First Christmas Poem: 1978

It's Christmas Eve and the hour is late,
It's the year of our Lord, one nine seven eight;
The tree is trimmed and the presents are spread,
All good kids are asleep in their bed.

The world seems still on this holiest of nights,
As nations pause with their quarrels and fights;
For on this night so long ago,
A Child was born, that the world would know
Peace on earth, good will toward men
Was the message He gave again and again.

We will listen from now 'til the first of the year,
And then His message we will not hear:
But hope everlasting the Lord gave to us,
Happy Birthday, Jesus.

Car Repair

Can you think of anything as bad as car repair
Getting there and getting back and getting treated fair
You know not what the troubles are
So come on in and leave your car
This is wrong and that is wrong, but we will have it done
By five o'clock tomorrow and bring us lots of "mon"

Sand and Sea

Oh what a day in life it can be
When you walk hand in hand with a friend by the sea
Sand 'tween your toes, the wind in your hair
Breathe all that you can of that fresh salty air
Shells you will find of every kind
Time, space and distance will fill up your mind
Cares that you have will seem far away
Time for them on another day

The day at the beach goes quickly by
The sun it seems, just falls from the sky
Oh what a day of blessings and joy
Too much to ask for this girl and boy
Back to our routine we will trudge
But one day again we will get the nudge
To go again by the sand and the sea
Where our hearts and our spirits are, oh, so free.

ABSOLUTES: no explanation needed

The rain falls.
The sun shines.
The earth spins.
The weatherman is wrong

A birthday poem for a friend, a graduate of Wake Forest....

>We know you're still pretty
>And we know you're not old
>But the card we are sending
>Should be the one that's called gold
>
>You're a great husband and father
>And to the rest you are a beacon
>So you are not doing bad
>For an old Demon Deacon

Out on the Range

Where can you find a cowboy
Well, you can find him out on the range
Don't ask a cowboy for a dollar
He doesn't even carry change
He don't get no snakebites
Because he wears his boots and chaps
And these days even some wear baseball caps
They save the "ten gallon" for when they go to town
And it's not like the movies
These days they don't tear the town down
They push cows and they work hard
And it's a living they are trying to make
Tell you when to think about a cowboy
The next time you eat a big juicy steak

A world without coffee

Why do you have to have coffee after something sweet
And sometimes you need it just to stay on your feet.
We have it in the morning, just to get awake
We have it at the office, just for coffee's sake
We could do without it-and the cakes and fritters
But in a world without it we all would have the jitters
So we will keep on drinking coffee and buy it by the pound
After all, it's coffee that makes the world go 'round

The black widow spider.

A spider was crawling in her web
Came upon a fly that sure was dead
She planted an egg in that fly
Gobbled up her husband and said, "good-by"
Later she was crawling by that fly
Something was moving and caught her eye
Baby spider is now alive
And crawling through the web
Looking for a fly

Reunion

It's fifty years since we've roamed those halls
And what do we remember
Youth, tradition and a way of life
And a school taking up in September

Visions, hopes and dreams we had
We even could reach for the sky
The Hilltop, the parks, the pool and such
And that school sitting there, West High

Some classmates and teachers no longer here
Will be remembered with fondness and tear
And even though the sky we didn't touch
We still love that school so very much

West High West High West High

Christmas comes but once a year,
A time for joy, a time for cheer.
Our spirits rise, we're full of joy,
We shower the kids with game and toy.
We love our neighbor as our brother,
We discover again our Dad and Mother.
We think of God, of Christ, of love,
We bow our heads and pray to Above,
For peace on earth, good will to men,
And then the season is gone again.
These things we know, that joy and cheer
They're gone again for another year.
That guy next door we called our neighbor,
Is the guy next door whose yard needs labor.
The love of God and Christ our Lord
Is still in our hearts but we have it stored.
The toys are broke and the kids didn't grasp
The meaning of the season that's just now past.
If only the time would come to us all,
When winter, summer, spring and fall
We'd feel these things the whole year through,
And that's what the Lord wants us to do

Life In the Pond.

The Tadpole

What happened to that tadpole
That tadpole now is gone
Where'd that frog come from
He jumped up, out of the pond
Where's that mosquito that was flying around
The frog done nailed him and gobbled him down
For that frog, I did scan
But he lost his legs to the frying pan
From that frying pan and into a body
Went the legs along with some toddy
This is the end of this here story
The next little bit would be too gory

The Grocery Store

When I go to the grocery store, I get in the shortest line.
I do that because my own time is my own time
It never fails and you know it too,
The longer lines get out before the shorter ones do.
I get a little basket and pretty soon it's full
Go get a great big cart, it's much easier to pull
I always take my coupons-do it to no avail
All those items just ran out because they were on sale.
We'll give you a "raincheck", but it will take a little while
We want you to leave our grocery, with on your face, a smile
I'm going home now—I'm on my way to my car.
I thought I parked it much closer but now it seems so far
Got to my car finally, and opened up the door,
Slammed some sacks on the back seat, some went on the floor.
Got home to my lovely wife—she smiled and said, "What's wrong?
You only went to the grocery store-whatever took you so long?"

A special Anniversary

We have been married for twenty-five years
We've had the ups and downs
And we've had the laughter and tears
We go to the future with our romance in place
We go to the future with God's love and grace

When I was a little critter....

I wanted to be a cowboy
And always thought I could
But my dad gave me a baseball
And a great big bat made of wood
I saddled up my broomstick
And rode off towards the west
My dad soon caught up with me
And told me, "Son, baseball is the best"
So baseball I will play
And play it with all of my might
But I'll dream about Hoppy, Gene and Roy
Almost every night.

A Cookie

What is it about a cookie
That sets you heart on fire?
It's sugary and it's fattening,
But of its taste, you'll never tire.
Mother made the best ones
And Gramma made them, too
But when you want a cookie
Any one will do.
So when you get that feeling
And your heart is beating fast
Go get a box of cookies
And see how long they last!

Puffins?

What in the world is a puffin
That name is so absurd.
I looked it up and to my amaze
It is nothing but a bird.
The young are fat, and so the puff
But it rhymes with almost nothin'
Just to be cute, they added "..in"
And now it rhymes with muffin.

My wife likes the comics and so ...

I brought you the thing in all the world
That I thought you needed the most
You have to have it on Sunday morn
To have with your tea and toast
You can have the world and all its gold
All of its jewels and monies
But how could you live for another week
If you missed the Sunday funnies

Another mall poem..... .

What do you see when you're in the mall
Besides all the pretty faces
There's every size and every shape
But of good taste, there's only traces
There's shop after shop, store after store
And a video arcade where you can score
You can even go and sit and look
You can even go and buy a book
There's this and more, so after all
If you've nothing to do, go to the mall

Taxes

We all have to pay our taxes
And it seems a terrible chore
We are sure we have paid in enough
But "oops", you owe some more
We all have to pay them, like it or not
Uncle Sam doesn't know how much money we've got
So be of good cheer and do not despair
And let's all pretend that taxes are fair.

CLUMSY FRIEND—broken arm

If you have to hurt
You might as well hurt your arm
It won't show up very much
And you can still retain your charm
If you happen to hurt your head
It probably will show
And if you hurt your leg
You may not be able to go
So keep on going for better or worse
And if it's at all possible
Stay close to a doctor and nurse.

Came the Wisemen
Came the Stranger
Came the Angels
To the manger
Your savior is born
They would say
On Him you believe
To Him you will pray
When the lights are lit
And the Christmas bell rings
Sing Hallelujah
To the King of Kings

Thanksgiving

How much turkey can we eat
And what do we have to prove
When we sit down at Thanksgiving
Knife, fork and spoon get in the groove
That's not what we sit down for
We're supposed to celebrate
We're supposed to give our thanks to God
Not see how much we ate
So thank you God, in heaven above
For food and drink and Your precious love

A Valentine to Sue

Happy Valentine's to you Sue, Sue
And thank you for all that you do, do
During these tough times we're going through
You keep me from getting too, too blue

Love, Glenn

For Mother's Day

Mothers are Moms and how great they are
Without them none of us would get very far
They fill our lives with love-sometimes a scold
They are there for us while young and as we grow old
This is you and I just want to say

I LOVE YOU—HAPPY MOTHER'S DAY

A Valentine

Valentine season is all about love
Including the love from Heaven above
So with the love, candy and romance
Let's give ourselves more than a chance
To spread God's Love all of the time
And wish the world: Happy Valentine

For Father's Day

Dear Father, dear Dad, dear Friend
The blessings you have given me will never end
This card is too small to put it all in
And I really don't know just where to begin
So I'll tell you I love you and just want to say
You're the best father ever-
    Happy Father's Day

DAUGHTER IN OHIO—
freezing

Nothing here is ever frozen
It has a better chance to melt
I know Ohio weather
For forty years I felt
There must be a happy medium
But no one knows where it's at
I guess between you and me
We'll keep wearing out the thermostat!
Be warm and happy all the time
And about the weather-don't bother
This comes from warm and dry Arizona
    With love-your Father

Any lady who has had a small kitchen..... .

My kitchen is small as kitchens go
Not much room for to and fro
But my kitchen has room for even a dance
If I get help with the dishes by chance
He goes that way and I go this
There even is room for a pat and a kiss
So I like my kitchen, just as it is
There's just enough room
For some "monkey biz"

A poem for a friend

Hannukka

Happy Holidays will not do
It's used too many times
A special card for my new friend
And one that surely rhymes
I hope your season is filled with cheer
So Happy Hannukka and a bright new year

A good friend lost his wife of forty years. They had been in love since high school. I wrote this poem for him to read at her graveside.

Memorial

Where are the pathways we used to roam
Where is that little house we used to call home
Where is that thing we had day to day
Where is that love that has fluttered away
Where is that future we used to plan
Where is that closeness of woman to man

They are all gone now. My Love has departed
I stand alone now as when we started
I will cherish our memories 'til the end of time
Rest easy my love I will always be thine

Decision

Hey you there—-the one who is walking thru life
Where are you going, what do you look for
Is your life full of love or full of strife
Many adjectives describe what we do
Is it good, is it bad, do we find anything that's true
What's next for you and what has life given
Will it be good, will it be bad, or mostly just livin'

Have you thought about God and what He can do
What's true is, He's just waiting for you
Me too, and all of mankind
To make a decision with heart, soul and mind
So keep on walking and walk a straight line
Surrender to Jesus and you will find
Where the truth is, where the love is
And why you are livin'
So make that decision and all is forgiven
Join the family and walk along with us
With God, Holy Spirit, and our Savior, Jesus

Christmas Friendship

There's many things we need in life
To ease the pain and ease the strife
One of these is one good friend
So knowing this, I'm going to send
A card that says you are the best
So Merry Christmas, and all the rest

The lights are on the Christmas tree
There are toys everywhere
The turkey is in the oven
And that smell is in the air
Our company is in the driveway
We just have heard their horn
And oh, by the way,

JESUS CHRIST WAS BORN

Christmas Present Time

The stockings are on the mantel
The lights are on the tree
The kids are on the stairway
Just where Dad can't see

The First Christmas

A stable they can sleep in
A manger where to lay
Miles and miles of hardships
Just for taxes they must pay

AND A CHILD WAS BORN
THAT THE WORLD WOULD KNOW

Merry Christmas

Merry Christmas in ninety-two
Happy New Year in ninety-three
Remember what God wants you to do
Remember what God wants you to be
He sent His Son to show us the way
This is the season of His birthday
The greatest of gifts was given to us
Humbly we say, "Happy Birthday, Jesus"

As we near the Christmas day,
Let's make sure our hearts are right,
Let us think of long ago,
When a heavenly star shone so bright.
Jesus came into the world
With all of His power and glory,
With gifts of joy and peace and love
Let us remember the Christmas story.

Merry Christmas

It's time to celebrate our Lord's birth
There's trouble it seems, all over the earth
Make sure we care at this Christmas time
I'll put it all in one simple rhyme.
Thank you, Lord God, for your saving Son
Thank you, Lord Jesus, oh, Holy One.

Merry Christmas

Onward they trudged into the night
Looking for a glimmer of Bethlehem's light.
No room at the inn, they were told
A stable and manger on a night so cold
Angels came and said do not fear
The Savior of the world soon would be here
All of Earth's Glory would come in this way
And Jesus our Lord is alive today

Merry Christmas

The night was cold and a star was bright
The angels came and they lit up the night
Jesus was born and salvation came
The world would bow and worship His name.
Thank you, Lord God, for that manger and stall
And a very merry Christmas, to one and all.

Jesus was born in the Holy Land
Son of God, Son of Man
He gave us the Word and showed us the way
He gave us the reason for Christmas Day
Thank you God for you blessed Son
And a Merry Christmas to everyone

Under a star that shone so bright
In a distant land on a cold, cold night
A child was born and the angels came
"This is your Savior, revere His name"
Thank you Lord, for that manger and stall
And a merry Christmas to one and all

Jesus lives on earth today
He will reign in heaven tomorrow
He brings love and joy into the world
He takes away sin and sorrow
He came to earth to save us all
So listen to our Savior's call

Merry Christmas

He came to us on Christmas day
Jesus our Lord, and He would say
Love you neighbor as yourself
Give up sin and give up wealth
His birth, His life, His sacrifice
Would open the doors to paradise
Let's remember on our Lord's Day
All He would do and
All He would say

Jesus lives in heaven above
Because of God's unending love
We're here on earth for the very same reason
And so we have the Christmas season
So with the presents, the joy and mirth
Please don't forget our Savior's birth

Merry Christmas

What is more free than a bird in the air
What is more captive than one who don't care
Let us all care at the Christmas time.
I've put it all in one simple rhyme
Thank you Lord God for your saving Son
Thank you Lord Jesus, oh, Holy One.

Merry Christmas

Jesus came because of God's grace
And His birthday now comes around
God blessed us so much at this time
Newton said it best "how sweet the sound"
And with the season and the hectic pace
Remember God's love, His Son, His grace

Remember 9-11-01

Peace on earth, good will to men
Are words we've heard again and again
Let's keep those words in our minds
While traveling thru these troubled times
And as we honor our Lord's birth
Let's pray once again for Peace on Earth

978-0-595-45333-7
0-595-45333-3

Printed in the United States
93574LV00001B/64-159/A